Ants and Beetles, Dragonflies

~ a child's guide to insects ~

by Susan Will

Book design: Rebecca & Diane Gaus

Illustrations by Charles Ettinger

Copyright © 2012 Susan Will

ISBN: 978-1-937129-24-8

Published by:
Faithful Life Publishers • North Fort Myers, FL 33903
www.FaithfulLifePublishers.com

info@FLPublishers.com

FREE Song track available at www.FaithfulLifePublishers.com
Bookstore ~ Children

Insects,

insects

have
six
legs.

They also have three body parts,

head and thorax,
abdomen.

Their
skeleton

is on the
outside.

ANTS
and

beetles,

dragonflies,

caterpillars,

butterflies!

Ants and Beetles, Dragonflies

Words: Susan Will

Music: "Twinkle, Twinkle, Litte Star"
Music Score: Glenn Christianson

FREE SONG DOWNLOAD

www.FaithfulLifePublishers.com • Bookstore ~ Children

Ants and Beetles, Dragonflies Song